2022:

A YEAR TO DECLUTTER LONG BEFORE YOU DOWNSIZE

IN THE HOME OF:

_____

_____

_____

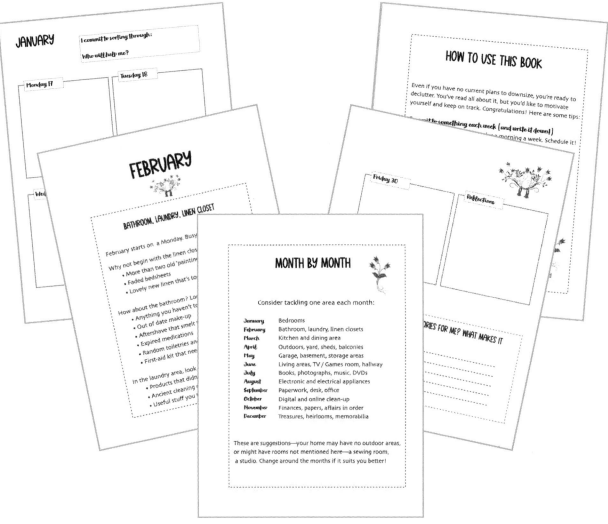

JANUARY

I commit to sorting through:

Who will help me?

Monday 17

Tuesday 18

FEBRUARY

BATHROOM, LAUNDRY, LINEN CLOSET

February starts on a Monday. Busy...

Why not begin with the linen clos...

- More than two old 'painting...
- Faded bedsheets
- Lovely new linen that's to...

How about the bathroom? Lo...

- Anything you haven't to...
- Out of date make-up
- Aftershave that smelt ...
- Expired medications
- Random toiletries an...
- First-aid kit that nee...

In the laundry area, look...

- Products that didn...
- Ancient cleaning ...
- Useful stuff you ...

HOW TO USE THIS BOOK

Even if you have no current plans to downsize, you're ready to declutter. You've read all about it, but you'd like to motivate yourself and keep on track. Congratulations! Here are some tips:

Commit to something each week (and write it down.)
...morning a week. Schedule it!

Friday 30

Reflections

MONTH BY MONTH

Consider tackling one area each month:

January	Bedrooms
February	Bathroom, laundry, linen closets
March	Kitchen and dining area
April	Outdoors, yard, sheds, balconies
May	Garage, basement, storage areas
June	Living areas, TV / Games room, hallway
July	Books, photographs, music, DVDs
August	Electronic and electrical appliances
September	Paperwork, desk, office
October	Digital and online clean-up
November	Finances, papers, affairs in order
December	Treasures, heirlooms, memorabilia

These are suggestions—your home may have no outdoor areas, or might have rooms not mentioned here—a sewing room, a studio. Change around the months if it suits you better!

...RIES FOR ME? WHAT MAKES IT

HOW TO USE THIS BOOK

Even if you have no current plans to downsize, you're ready to declutter. You've read all about it, but you'd like to motivate yourself and keep on track. Congratulations! Here are some tips:

Commit to something each week (and write it down!)

It could be 15 minutes a day, plus a morning a week. Schedule it! Then keep a note of what you've done each day.

Get a buddy and plan ahead

Why not find a friend who also wants to declutter?
You could trade a morning of support for each other.
If you can't meet in person, how about online?
SAFETY TIP: Get help if lifting heavy items, plus take regular breaks. It's easy to get carried away.

Take photos

Each month, take 'before and after' photos of rooms.
Include the inside of closets and drawers.
Share with your buddy and enjoy the difference.

Reflect and appreciate

Take time to appreciate both the things you're keeping and the things you're letting go.

WHAT DO I DO WITH STUFF I DON'T NEED?

Think about this before you start…

Alert the family, if you have one

True, they may never have shown an interest, but give them the chance to refuse their old bedroom furniture.

In particular, always check before you let go of THEIR stuff.

Make a video call if they need a reminder of what they've left with you. Box up all the things they beg you to keep.

Plan ahead

Give away or sell? It can be easier to let go if you know that any valuable things are going to a worthy home:

- A local charity or shelter?
- A 'buying nothing' community group?
- The local pet shelter? (old towels and fleece blankets)
- A local school? (craft items)

Think eco-friendly

Find out where you can safely dispose of:

- Chemicals, paint, insecticides
- Expired medications
- Electronic goods (ensure all memory is wiped)
- Goods that might be unsafe (ancient cots, car seats)

MONTH BY MONTH

Consider tackling one area each month:

January	Bedrooms
February	Bathroom, laundry, linen closets
March	Kitchen and dining area
April	Outdoors, yard, sheds, balconies
May	Garage, basement, storage areas
June	Living areas, TV / Games room, hallway
July	Books, photographs, music, DVDs
August	Electronic and electrical appliances
September	Paperwork, desk, office
October	Digital and online clean-up
November	Finances, papers, affairs in order
December	Treasures, heirlooms, memorabilia

These are suggestions—your home may have no outdoor areas, or might have rooms not mentioned here—a sewing room, a studio. Change around the months if it suits you better!

2022

JANUARY

SU	MO	TU	WE	TH	FR	SA
						1
2	3	4	5	6	7	8
9	10	11	12	13	14	15
16	17	18	19	20	21	22
23	24	25	26	27	28	29
30	31					

FEBRUARY

SU	MO	TU	WE	TH	FR	SA
		1	2	3	4	5
6	7	8	9	10	11	12
13	14	15	16	17	18	19
20	21	22	23	24	25	26
27	28					

MARCH

SU	MO	TU	WE	TH	FR	SA
		1	2	3	4	5
6	7	8	9	10	11	12
13	14	15	16	17	18	19
20	21	22	23	24	25	26
27	28	29	30	31		

APRIL

SU	MO	TU	WE	TH	FR	SA
					1	2
3	4	5	6	7	8	9
10	11	12	13	14	15	16
17	18	19	20	21	22	23
24	25	26	27	28	29	30

MAY

SU	MO	TU	WE	TH	FR	SA
1	2	3	4	5	6	7
8	9	10	11	12	13	14
15	16	17	18	19	20	21
22	23	24	25	26	27	28
29	30	31				

JUNE

SU	MO	TU	WE	TH	FR	SA
			1	2	3	4
5	6	7	8	9	10	11
12	13	14	15	16	17	18
19	20	21	22	23	24	25
26	27	28	29	30		

NOTES

2022

JULY

SU	MO	TU	WE	TH	FR	SA
					1	2
3	4	5	6	7	8	9
10	11	12	13	14	15	16
17	18	19	20	21	22	23
24	25	26	27	28	29	30
31						

AUGUST

SU	MO	TU	WE	TH	FR	SA
	1	2	3	4	5	6
7	8	9	10	11	12	13
14	15	16	17	18	19	20
21	22	23	24	25	26	27
28	29	30	31			

SEPTEMBER

SU	MO	TU	WE	TH	FR	SA
				1	2	3
4	5	6	7	8	9	10
11	12	13	14	15	16	17
18	19	20	21	22	23	24
25	26	27	28	29	30	

OCTOBER

SU	MO	TU	WE	TH	FR	SA
						1
2	3	4	5	6	7	8
9	10	11	12	13	14	15
16	17	18	19	20	21	22
23	24	25	26	27	28	29
30	31					

NOVEMBER

SU	MO	TU	WE	TH	FR	SA
		1	2	3	4	5
6	7	8	9	10	11	12
13	14	15	16	17	18	19
20	21	22	23	24	25	26
27	28	29	30			

DECEMBER

SU	MO	TU	WE	TH	FR	SA
				1	2	3
4	5	6	7	8	9	10
11	12	13	14	15	16	17
18	19	20	21	22	23	24
25	26	27	28	29	30	31

NOTES

2022

MY VISION FOR THIS HOME

JANUARY

STARTING SIMPLY: IN THE BEDROOMS

Start simply, with a bedroom round-up.

Look for things like:
- What no longer looks right/doesn't fit
- Gifts you've never worn
- Odd socks, old or stained items
- Drawers and cupboards stuffed full
- Old, lumpy pillows
- Storage containers on top of cupboards
- Things under beds

What can you do with the things you don't need?

TIP: Also check safety and emergency supplies, like smoke alarms and flashlights.

JANUARY

I commit to sorting through:

Who will help me:

MY VISION FOR JANUARY:

THINGS TO DO, PEOPLE TO CONTACT:

Let's get started!

Saturday 1

- Annual perge of bills & receipts

- Sort out coathangers

Sunday 2

- Sort out man cupboard

Reflections

JANUARY

I commit to sorting through:

Who will help me?

Monday 3

- Put away xmas decorations
- Sort old decorations

Tuesday 4

- Clear undersink
- Plan a daily kitchen routine

Wednesday 5

- Clear kitchen surfaces

Thursday 6

- Clean kick boards

Friday 7

- Clean & sort kitchen dresser.

Saturday 8

- Sort tea towels, kitchen towels, aprons & oven gloves.

Sunday 9

- clear fireplace

Reflections

- Take stuff to Charity Shop

JANUARY

I commit to sorting through:

Who will help me?

Monday 10

- Sort wall cabinets

Tuesday 11

- Sort kitchen drawers

Wednesday 12

- Sort base units - kitchen

Thursday 13

- Declutter tall cupboard

Friday 14

- Declutter food containers

Saturday 15

Sunday 16

Reflections

- Take stuff to charity shop

JANUARY

I commit to sorting through:

Who will help me?

Monday 17

Tuesday 18

Wednesday 19

Thursday 20

Friday 21

Saturday 22

Sunday 23

Reflections

JANUARY

I commit to sorting through:

Who will help me?

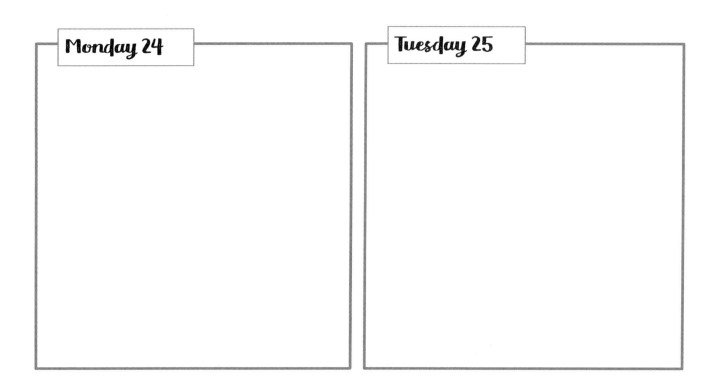

Monday 24

Tuesday 25

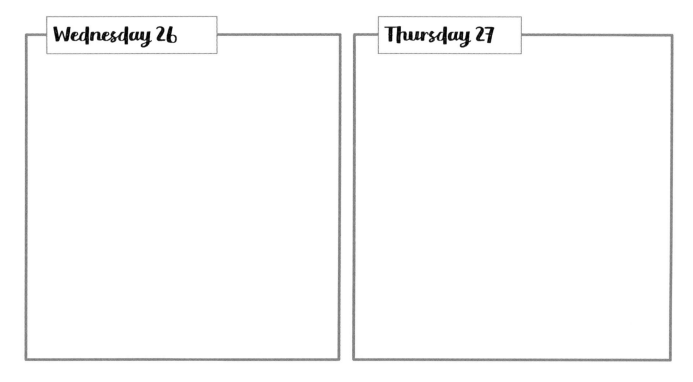

Wednesday 26

Thursday 27

Friday 28

Saturday 29

Sunday 30

Mon 31

JANUARY
SUCCESSES

FEBRUARY

BATHROOM, LAUNDRY, LINEN CLOSET

Busy? Start small.

Why not begin with the linen closet? Look for:
- More than two old 'painting' towels
- Faded bedsheets
- Lovely new linen that's too good to use (use it!)

How about the bathroom? Look for things like:
- Anything you haven't touched in a year
- Out of date make-up
- Aftershave that smelt too strong
- Expired medications
- Random toiletries and half-full bottles
- First-aid kit that needs updating

In the laundry area, look for:
- Products that didn't work so well
- Ancient cleaning cloths
- Useful stuff you thought you'd lost

FEBRUARY

I commit to sorting through:

Who will help me?

MY VISION FOR FEBRUARY:

Step by Step!

THINGS I NEED, TO IMPROVE MY STORAGE:

FEBRUARY

I commit to sorting through:

Who will help me?

Ideas

Tuesday 1 Feb

Wednesday 2

Thursday 3

Friday 4

Saturday 5

Sunday 6

Reflections

FEBRUARY

I commit to sorting through:

Who will help me?

| Monday 7 | Tuesday 8 |

| Wednesday 9 | Thursday 10 |

Friday 11

Saturday 12

Sunday 13

Reflections

FEBRUARY

I commit to sorting through:

Who will help me?

Monday 14	Tuesday 15

Wednesday 16	Thursday 17

Friday 18

Saturday 19

Sunday 20

Reflections

FEBRUARY

I commit to sorting through:

Who will help me?

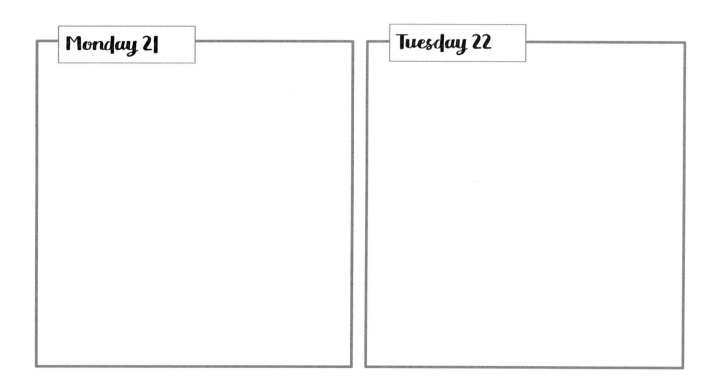

Monday 21

Tuesday 22

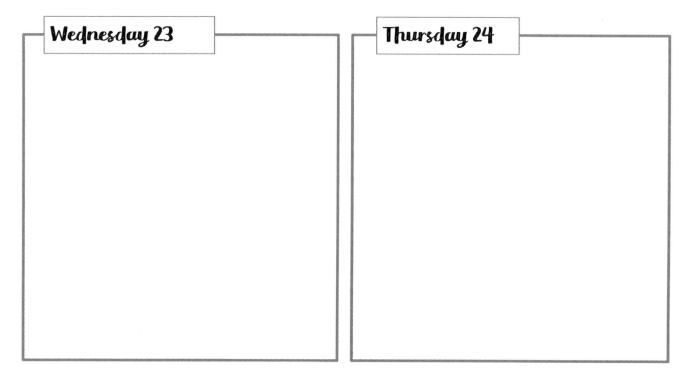

Wednesday 23

Thursday 24

Friday 25

Saturday 26

Sunday 27

Monday 28

FEBRUARY
SUCCESSES

MARCH

IN THE KITCHEN, DINING AREA

Again, start small if you're busy.

Begin in the kitchen, with the pantry or food cupboard:
- Sort through dry food cans and packs
- Look for expired items, things hidden at the back
- Rotate emergency supplies

Then the drawers and cupboards. Look for things like:
- Plates and cups you don't like
- Old mixers and egg poachers
- Spare glasses for massive parties
- Things hidden at the back of corner cupboards
- Stuff you'd forgotten about
- More than 6 shopping bags

How about the dining area? Look for things like:
- More drawers stuffed full
- Tablecloths you don't love
- Candlesticks you don't use

MARCH

I commit to sorting through:

Who will help me?

MY VISION FOR MARCH:

WHAT IS LOVELY BUT UNNECESSARY IN MY LIFE NOW?
WHO MIGHT LIKE IT?

PLACES THAT ACCEPT USED GOODS:

MARCH

I commit to sorting through:

Who will help me?

Ideas

Tuesday 1 Mar

Wednesday 2

Thursday 3

Friday 4

Saturday 5

Sunday 6

Reflections

MARCH

I commit to sorting through:

Who will help me?

Monday 7	Tuesday 8

Wednesday 9	Thursday 10

Friday 11

Saturday 12

Sunday 13

Reflections

MARCH

I commit to sorting through:

Who will help me?

Monday 14

Tuesday 15

Wednesday 16

Thursday 17

Friday 18

Saturday 19

Sunday 20

Reflections

MARCH

I commit to sorting through:

Who will help me?

Monday 21	Tuesday 22

Wednesday 23	Thursday 24

Friday 25

Saturday 26

Sunday 27

Reflections

MARCH

I commit to sorting through:

Who will help me?

Monday 28

Tuesday 29

Wednesday 30

Thursday 31

AM I ABLE TO ENJOY THE PROCESS OF LETTING GO?
IS THERE MORE LETTING GO FOR ME TO DO?

HOW DO I FEEL ABOUT MY HOME NOW?

MARCH
SUCCESSES

APRIL

OUTDOORS, YARD, SHEDS, BALCONIES

Walk around outside and visit any outdoor storage.

Look for things like:

- Old gardening tools
- Broken garden ornaments
- Old pots full of spiders
- Paint that matched your walls in 2007
- Rusty tools that don't cut or saw properly
- Anything saved 'just in case' for over 3 years
- Plastic storage crates full of odd stuff
- Outdoor furniture that wobbles
- Trip hazards

You know what to do next…

APRIL

I commit to sorting through:

Who will help me?

MY VISION FOR APRIL:

Friday 1

Saturday 2

Sunday 3

Reflections

APRIL

I commit to sorting through:

Who will help me?

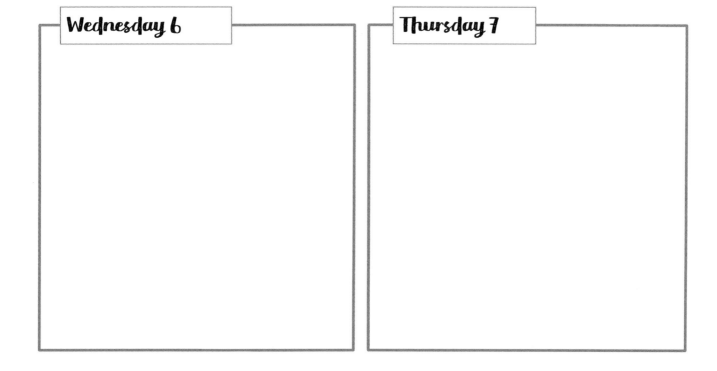

Monday 4

Tuesday 5

Wednesday 6

Thursday 7

Friday 8

Saturday 9

Sunday 10

Reflections

APRIL

I commit to sorting through:

Who will help me?

Monday 11

Tuesday 12

Wednesday 13

Thursday 14

Friday 15

Saturday 16

Sunday 17

Reflections

APRIL

I commit to sorting through:

Who will help me?

Monday 18

Tuesday 19

Wednesday 20

Thursday 21

Friday 22

Saturday 23

Sunday 24

Reflections

APRIL

I commit to sorting through:

Who will help me?

Monday 25

Tuesday 26

Wednesday 27

Thursday 28

Friday 29

Saturday 30

WHAT OBJECTS HOLD MEMORIES FOR ME? WHAT MAKES IT HARD TO LET GO?

APRIL
SUCCESSES

MAY

GARAGE, BASEMENT, STORAGE AREAS

It's May! We're looking at more storage areas: basements, attics, under the stairs. Look for:

- Old furniture that's 'too good' to throw out
- Paintings you don't like
- Sports gear you don't use
- Things you're storing for family members
- Plastic crates full of useful stuff
- Old hobby supplies (last touched in 2007)
- Magazines, manuals from long-gone appliances

Ask yourself:

- Who do I need to ask about their stuff?
- Can I send them a photo to remind them?
- Who else in the family might like my things?
- What charities or shelters would I like to support?

This is an area where it's REALLY good to have help.

MAY

I commit to sorting through:

Who will help me?

MY VISION FOR MAY:

It feels so spacious!

Ideas

Sunday 1

Reflections

MAY

I commit to sorting through:

Who will help me?

Monday 2	Tuesday 3

Wednesday 4	Thursday 5

Friday 6

Saturday 7

Sunday 8

Reflections

MAY

I commit to sorting through:

Who will help me?

Monday 9

Tuesday 10

Wednesday 11

Thursday 12

Friday 13

Saturday 14

Sunday 15

Reflections

MAY

I commit to sorting through:

Who will help me?

Monday 16	Tuesday 17

Wednesday 18	Thursday 19

Friday 20

Saturday 20

Sunday 22

Reflections

MAY

I commit to sorting through:

Who will help me?

Monday 23

Tuesday 24

Wednesday 25

Thursday 26

Friday 27

Saturday 28

Sunday 29

Reflections

MAY

I commit to sorting through:

Who will help me?

Monday 30	Tuesday 31

MAY SUCCESSES

JUNE

LIVING AREAS, TV ROOM, GAMES ROOM, HALLWAY

You probably know what you need to sort in the living areas and in the entry or hallway.

Look for:

- Ornaments on display that you don't like
- Anything that doesn't have meaning for you
- Things with bad memories or associations
- Faded throws or cushions
- Stuffed toys, board games you don't play
- Drawers of assorted bits and pieces
- Objects you don't like dusting
- Old magazines
- Old coffee table books (books are next month)

No need to be minimalist – unless you want to!
Just surround yourself with things you love.

JUNE

I commit to sorting through:

Who will help me?

MY VISION FOR JUNE:

HOW GOOD IS IT TO KNOW THAT SOMEONE IS GETTING DELIGHT FROM THINGS I NO LONGER NEED?

HAVE I MISSED ANYTHING I LET GO OF EARLIER THIS YEAR?

JUNE

I commit to sorting through:

Who will help me?

Enjoy letting go!

Ideas

Wednesday 1

Thursday 2

Friday 3

Saturday 4

Sunday 5

Reflections

JUNE

I commit to sorting through:

Who will help me?

Monday 6

Tuesday 7

Wednesday 8

Thursday 9

Friday 10

Saturday 11

Sunday 12

Reflections

JUNE

I commit to sorting through:

Who will help me?

Monday 13	Tuesday 14

Wednesday 15	Thursday 16

Friday 17

Saturday 18

Sunday 19

Reflections

JUNE

I commit to sorting through:

Who will help me?

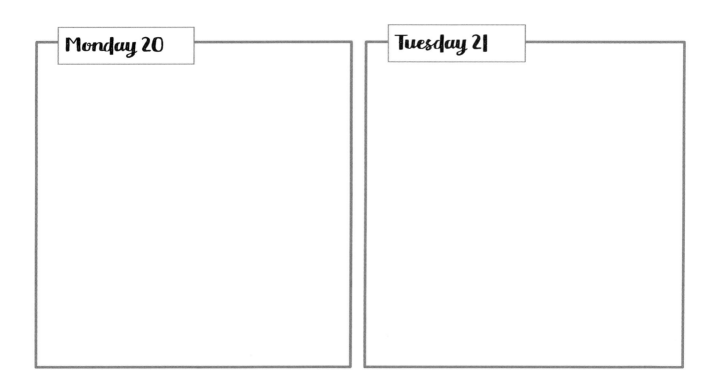

Monday 20

Tuesday 21

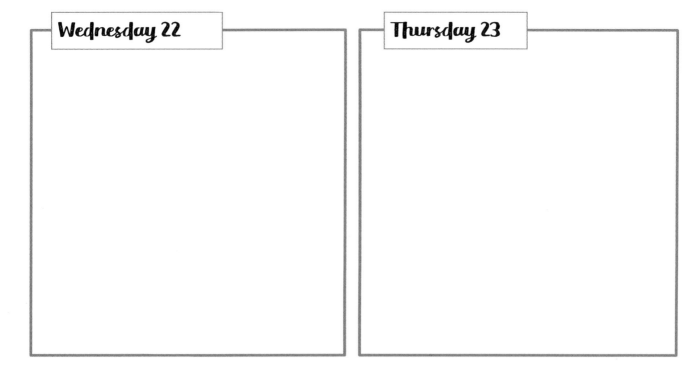

Wednesday 22

Thursday 23

Friday 24

Saturday 25

Sunday 26

Reflections

JUNE

I commit to sorting through:

Who will help me?

Monday 27	Tuesday 28

Wednesday 29	Thursday 30

JUNE
SUCCESSES

HALF-WAY!
MY THOUGHTS SO FAR

JULY

BOOKS, PHOTOGRAPHS, MUSIC, DVDS

Look at your bookshelves and ask yourself:
- What would I buy again in a heartbeat?
- What would I like to pass on to others?
- Have I asked the kids about their old books?
- Is there anything vintage or valuable?

Look at old photo albums and check:
- Are the photos labelled?
- Does anything need to be restored or framed?
- Could I get them stored digitally?
- Do I have other collectibles like stamps or coins?
- Do they need to be valued? Stored properly?

Look at DVDs, videos, CDs, film, records, cassettes. Ask:
- Can I still watch or listen? Will I?
- Do I need to get these stored in another format?

JULY

I commit to sorting through:

Who will help me?

MY VISION FOR JULY:

Friday 1

Saturday 2

Sunday 3

Reflections

JULY

I commit to sorting through:

Who will help me?

Monday 4

Tuesday 5

Wednesday 6

Thursday 7

Friday 8

Saturday 9

Sunday 10

Reflections

JULY

I commit to sorting through:

Who will help me?

Monday 11

Tuesday 12

Wednesday 13

Thursday 14

Friday 15

Saturday 16

Sunday 17

Reflections

JULY

I commit to sorting through:

Who will help me?

Monday 18

Tuesday 19

Wednesday 20

Thursday 21

Friday 22

Saturday 23

Sunday 24

Reflections

JULY

I commit to sorting through:

Who will help me?

Monday 25

Tuesday 26

Wednesday 27

Thursday 28

Friday 29

Saturday 30

Sunday 31

I'm getting there!

JULY
SUCCESSES

- -

- -

- -

- -

- -

- -

- -

- -

- -

- -

- -

AUGUST

ELECTRONIC & ELECTRICAL APPLIANCES

This month, look all over the house for things like:
- Drawers full of random cords
- Old VCR units, slide projectors
- Old phones, toys which once had batteries
- Earlier models of things you own
- That 2005 computer and all the floppy disks

Ask yourself:
- What do I actually need and use?
- What could I move along? Who would take it?
- Would they need to check it out for safety?
- Can I dispose of this safely?
- How will I make sure my data is wiped?
- How can I store and label what's left?

AUGUST

I commit to sorting through:

Who will help me?

MY VISION FOR AUGUST:

AM I BEING MORE THOUGHTFUL ABOUT WHAT I PURCHASE?

AM I FINDING THE PERFECT WAY TO PASS THINGS ON?

AUGUST

I commit to sorting through:

Who will help me?

Monday 1

Tuesday 2

Wednesday 3

Thursday 4

Friday 5

Saturday 6

Sunday 7

Reflections

AUGUST

I commit to sorting through:

Who will help me?

Monday 8

Tuesday 9

Wednesday 10

Thursday 11

Friday 12

Saturday 13

Sunday 14

Reflections

AUGUST

I commit to sorting through:

Who will help me?

Monday 15	Tuesday 16

Wednesday 17	Thursday 18

Friday 19

Saturday 20

Sunday 21

Reflections

AUGUST

I commit to sorting through:

Who will help me?

Monday 22

Tuesday 23

Wednesday 24

Thursday 25

Friday 26

Saturday 27

Sunday 28

Reflections

AUGUST

I commit to sorting through:

Who will help me?

Monday 29

Tuesday 30

Wednesday 31

It's all worth it!

WHAT DID I FIND THAT I HAD FORGOTTEN ABOUT?

WHAT DO I REALISE I MOST VALUE?

AUGUST
SUCCESSES

SEPTEMBER

PAPERWORK, DESK, OFFICE, FILES, DRAWERS

This month is a 'desk, office, paperwork' month.
(If you don't have a shredder, borrow one!)

Look for things like:
- Tax receipts that no longer need to be kept
- Other receipts from 2001
- Drawers full of dried up pens
- Trays full of stuff 'to read' and 'to file'
- Family history that needs to be organised
- Anything that could be scanned and digitised

TIP: Have you got your key documents in a small home safe or portable fireproof safe?

QUESTION: Could someone come in and easily find what they need, if you had a short 'health episode'?

SEPTEMBER

I commit to sorting through:

Who will help me?

MY VISION FOR SEPTEMBER

More thoughts

Thursday 1

Friday 2

Saturday 3

Sunday 4

Reflections

SEPTEMBER

I commit to sorting through:

Who will help me?

Monday 5

Tuesday 6

Wednesday 7

Thursday 8

Friday 9

Saturday 10

Sunday 11

Reflections

SEPTEMBER

I commit to sorting through:

Who will help me?

Monday 12

Tuesday 13

Wednesday 14

Thursday 15

Friday 16

Saturday 17

Sunday 18

Reflections

SEPTEMBER

I commit to sorting through:

Who will help me?

Monday 19

Tuesday 20

Wednesday 21

Thursday 22

Friday 23

Saturday 24

Sunday 25

Reflections

SEPTEMBER

I commit to sorting through:

Who will help me?

Monday 26	Tuesday 27

Wednesday 28	Thursday 29

Friday 30

Reflections

HOW SPACIOUS DOES EVERYTHING FEEL NOW?

....

....

....

HOW CAN I MAINTAIN THIS?

....

....

....

SEPTEMBER
SUCCESSES

OCTOBER

DIGITAL AND ONLINE CLEAN-UP

How tidy is your digital life? Are there any:

- Mailing lists you should unsubscribe from?
- Emails that need deleting (or storing in folders)?
- Files cluttering your downloads or desktop?
- Documents that are hard to find?
- Duplicate photos?
- Security settings on social media to be tweaked?

TIP: Is a copy of your password list in the home safe?

TIP: This isn't a physically active clean-up, so remember to keep moving!

OCTOBER

I commit to sorting through:

Who will help me?

MY VISION FOR OCTOBER

Pleased with myself!

Saturday 1

Sunday 2

Reflections

OCTOBER

I commit to sorting through:

Who will help me?

Monday 3

Tuesday 4

Wednesday 5

Thursday 6

Friday 7

Saturday 8

Sunday 9

Reflections

OCTOBER

I commit to sorting through:

Who will help me?

Monday 10

Tuesday 11

Wednesday 12

Thursday 13

Friday 14

Saturday 15

Sunday 16

Reflections

OCTOBER

I commit to sorting through:

Who will help me?

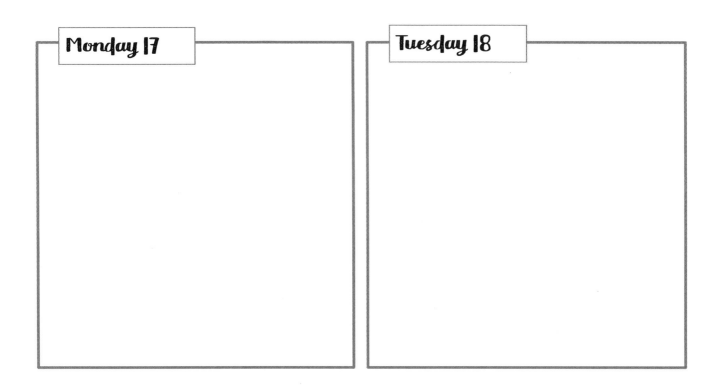

Monday 17	Tuesday 18

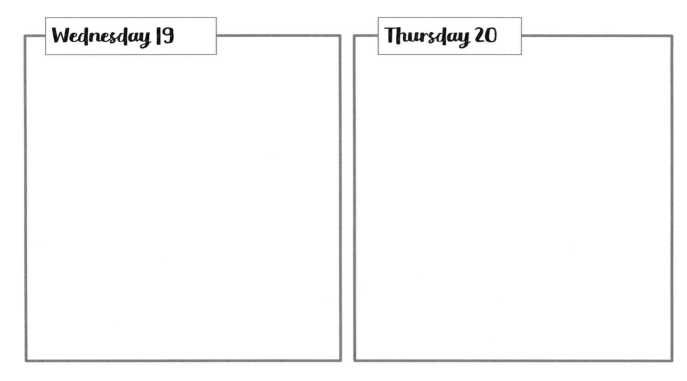

Wednesday 19	Thursday 20

Friday 21

Saturday 22

Sunday 23

Reflections

OCTOBER

I commit to sorting through:

Who will help me?

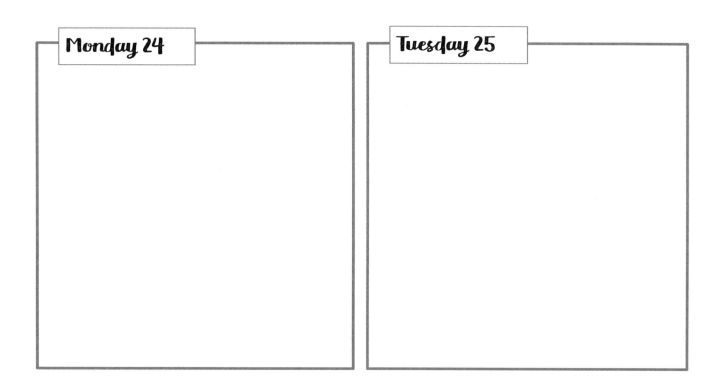

Monday 24	Tuesday 25

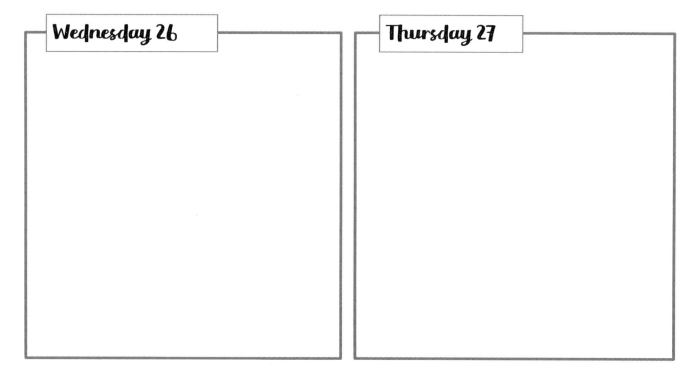

Wednesday 26	Thursday 27

Friday 28

Saturday 29

Sunday 30

Monday 31

OCTOBER
SUCCESSES

NOVEMBER

FINANCES, PAPERS AND AFFAIRS IN ORDER

You could start this month with some reflection and planning. Some of this month's work could be confronting –– the 'just in case' scenario.

You're going to check that your finances and papers are all in order. Can you create lists of:

- Investments, bank accounts, income streams
- Subscriptions and recurring payments
- Regular bills and payments
- Regular jobs that need doing

Where is your will? Is your living will or advance care directive also stored where it's easy to find?

On a cheerier note, why not update:
- Address book and holiday card list
- List of 'people to call', trade services etc

NOVEMBER

I commit to sorting through:

Who will help me?

MY VISION FOR NOVEMBER

Look how far I've come!

Notes

HOW CAN I 'BE PREPARED' IN A POSITIVE WAY?'

NOVEMBER

I commit to sorting through:

Who will help me?

Notes	Tuesday 1 Nov

Wednesday 2	Thursday 3

Friday 4

Saturday 5

Sunday 6

Reflections

NOVEMBER

I commit to sorting through:

Who will help me?

Monday 7	Tuesday 8

Wednesday 9	Thursday 10

Friday 11

Saturday 12

Sunday 13

Reflections

NOVEMBER

I commit to sorting through:

Who will help me?

Monday 14

Tuesday 15

Wednesday 16

Thursday 17

Friday 18

Saturday 19

Sunday 20

Reflections

NOVEMBER

I commit to sorting through:

Who will help me?

Monday 21	Tuesday 22

Wednesday 23	Thursday 24

Friday 25

Saturday 26

Sunday 27

Reflections

NOVEMBER

I commit to sorting through:

Who will help me?

Monday 28

Tuesday 29

Wednesday 30

So much that's done!

WHAT DO I NOW FEEL REALLY GOOD ABOUT?

DO I NEED TO DISCUSS THIS WITH ANYONE?

NOVEMBER
SUCCESSES

DECEMBER

TREASURES, HEIRLOOMS & MEMORABILIA

It's December! Just a month to go. This month, why not focus on things that mean a lot to you?

Look through storage tubs, boxes, drawers and cabinets, at memorabilia and treasures.

These could be valuable, or of sentimental value, like old birthday cards.

No pressure to let go of anything, but ask yourself:
- Am I enjoying these treasures?
- Are they stored or displayed well?
- Are there alternative ways to store them?
- Do I have a long-term plan for them?
- What would I take to the ends of the earth?
- Do I feel surrounded by things I love?

DECEMBER

I commit to sorting through:

Who will help me?

MY VISION FOR DECEMBER

More thoughts

Thursday I

Friday 2

Saturday 3

Sunday 4

Reflections

DECEMBER

I commit to sorting through:

Who will help me?

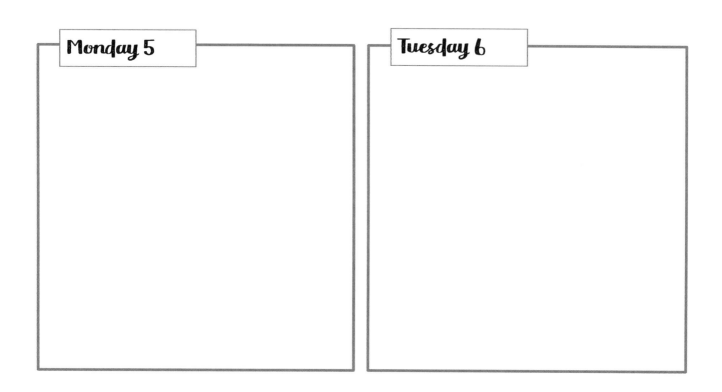

Monday 5

Tuesday 6

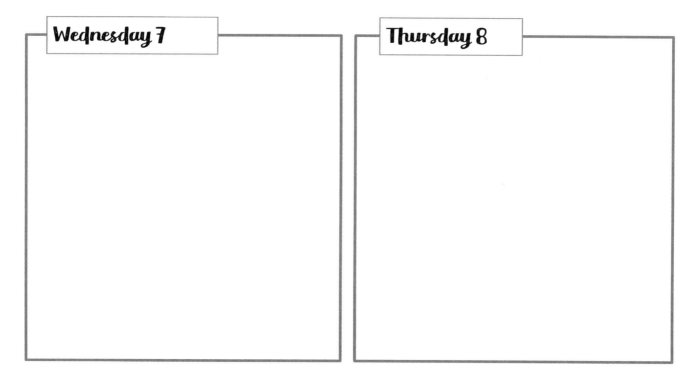

Wednesday 7

Thursday 8

Friday 9

Saturday 10

Sunday 11

Reflections

DECEMBER

I commit to sorting through:

Who will help me?

Monday 12

Tuesday 13

Wednesday 14

Thursday 15

Friday 16

Saturday 17

Sunday 18

Reflections

DECEMBER

I commit to sorting through:

Who will help me?

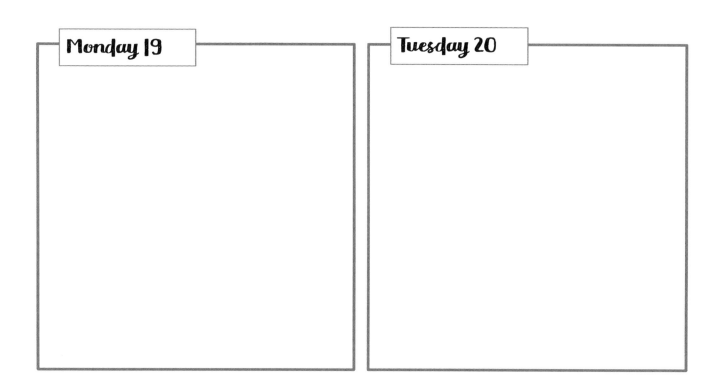

Monday 19

Tuesday 20

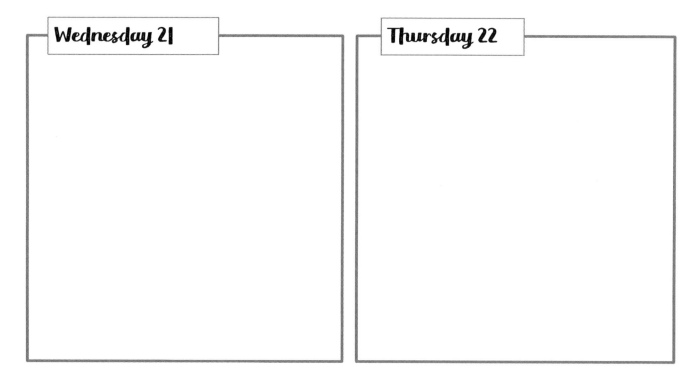

Wednesday 21

Thursday 22

Friday 23

Saturday 24

Sunday 25

Reflections

DECEMBER

I commit to sorting through:

Who will help me?

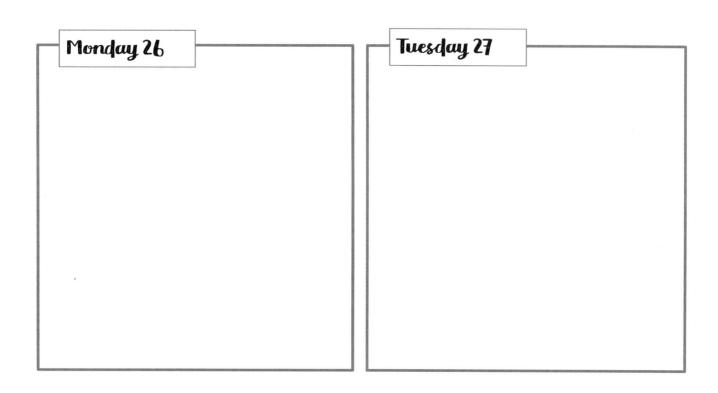

Monday 26

Tuesday 27

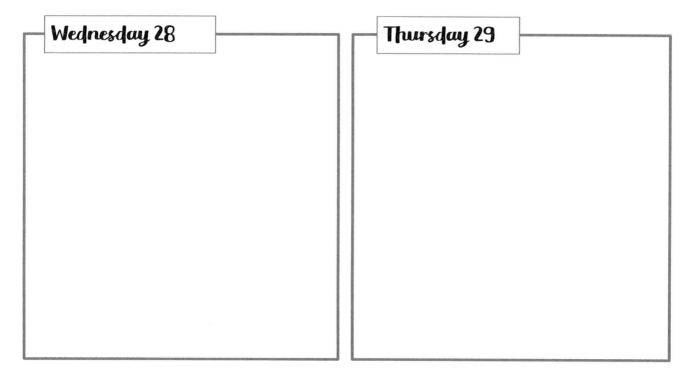

Wednesday 28

Thursday 29

Friday 30

Saturday 31

What a
year!

MY FEELINGS NOW...

- -
- -
- -
- -
- -

DECEMBER
SUCCESSES

HOW CAN I TRULY CELEBRATE ALL MY SUCCESSES?

2022

MY HOME IN REVIEW

2023

WHAT'S NEXT?

Wishing you a happy and clutter-free year, every year!

Thanks also to iriana88w, Marisha and NadejdaEmelyanova at Deposit Photos.